B·I·B·L·E WORLD

THE LIFE THAT CHANGED THE WORLD

For Alethea

MO

Copyright © 1994 Lion Publishing

First published in the United States of America in 1994 by Thomas Nelson, Inc., Publishers, Nashville, Tennessee, and distributed in Canada by Word Communications, Ltd., Richmond, British Colombia

Text by John Drane

The author asserts the moral right
to be identified as the author of this work

Published by
Lion Publishing plc
Sandy Lane West, Oxford, England
ISBN 0 7459 2174 4
Albatross Books Pty Ltd
PO Box 320, Sutherland, NSW 2232, Australia
ISBN 0 7324 0544 0

Contributors to this volume
John Drane is Director of the Center for the Study of Christianity and Contemporary Society at the University of Stirling and the author of several highly acclaimed books on the Bible and its background. In this book he presents the Bible and its history in a way that young people can understand and enjoy.

Alan Millard, Rankin Professor of Hebrew and Ancient Semitic Languages at Liverpool University, is the consultant for the illustrations in this book, and all the books in the series.

Acknowledgments
All photographs are copyright © Lion Publishing, except the following:
Ancient Art and Architecture Collection: 2 (above right);
Susanna Burton: 11 (above right), 15 (below left);
Zefa: 14 (far right), 20 (below left).

The following Lion Publishing photographs appear by courtesy of:
the Biblical Resources Pilgrim Center, Tantur: 4 (below right), 13 (middle right);
the Eretz Israel Museum, Tel Aviv: 19 (below left).

Illustrations, copyright © Lion Publishing, by:
Chris Molan: 1, 2 (above left and below right), 3, 4, 5 (above), 6, 7, 8, 9, 10, 11, 12 (below), 13, 14, 15, 16 (above), 17, 18 (left), 19, 20;
Jeffrey Burn: 1 (below left), 2 (below left), 5 (below left), 12 (above right), 16 (below right), 18 (below right).

Maps, copyright © Lion Publishing, by:
Oxford Illustrators Ltd: 1, 2, 6, 8, 20.

Bible quotations are taken from the Good News Bible, copyright © American Bible Society, New York, 1966, 1971 and 4th edition 1976, published by the Bible Societies/Harper Collins, with permission.

Story text is based on material from *The Lion Children's Bible*, by Pat Alexander

ISBN 0-7852-7997-0

Printed and bound in Malaysia

1 2 3 4 5—98 97 96 95 94

THE LIFE THAT CHANGED THE WORLD

THE STORY OF JESUS

John Drane

THOMAS NELSON PUBLISHERS
Nashville • Atlanta • London • Vancouver

Contents

1 The Time Before Jesus

2 The Romans

3 Waiting for a King

4 The Birth Day

5 King Herod and the Wise Men

6 At Home in Nazareth

7 Special Assignment

8 A New Kind of Teacher

9 New Power

10 The New Kingdom

page 13

page 13

page 13

page 1

page 2

7.99

11 Jesus Shares a Secret

12 The Healer

13 Who Was This Man?

14 The Good News

15 Friends and Enemies

16 The Triumphant King

17 Betrayed

18 A Day of Darkness

19 Alive Again!

20 An End and a Beginning

page 5

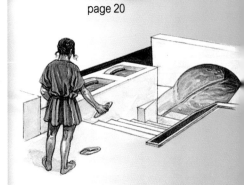
page 20

page 15

page 9

page 14

page 17

1 The Time Before Jesus

Jesus is one of the most remarkable people who ever lived. He was a Jew who lived 2,000 years ago, in a small town in Palestine. He was not particularly famous in his own time, and he died in unusual circumstances.

Yet he is at the heart of Christianity. Throughout history, people have been inspired by his teaching and example.

▼ **Greek Empire**
Alexander's empire spread eastward from Greece to the borders of north India.

Greeks and Jews

The recent history of the Jews had been one long, sorry tale of invasion and oppression by other nations.

In just ten years, from 333 to 323 B.C., the Greek ruler Alexander the Great created an enormous empire. He was less cruel than many dictators—although he believed Greek ways of doing things were the best, he did allow other nations to continue their old ways of life. But he insisted they should speak Greek and learn about Greek culture—things such as the athletic games, the theater, philosophy and literature.

When Alexander died, his four generals divided the empire. For a while, things continued as before. Then Antiochus IV became king in 175 B.C.. He forced the Jews to live like Greeks, and put his religion in the place of theirs. Anyone who resisted was put to death.

Led by the family of the Maccabees, a Jewish resistance movement began to fight Antiochus in 168 B.C., and within three years they had won. Never again would a foreign ruler be able to force the Jewish people to abandon their faith and way of life.

▶ **Freedom fighter**
The Jewish freedom fighter Judas Maccabeus was horrified to find an altar to foreign gods at the heart of God's temple in Jerusalem.

▼ **Foreign rule**
By the time of Jesus, the Jews in Palestine had been under foreign rule for over 300 years.

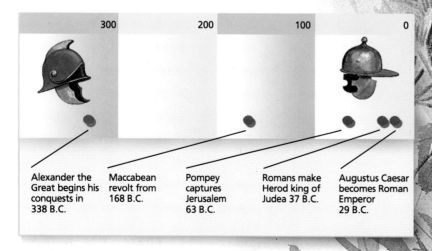

Alexander the Great begins his conquests in 338 B.C.

Maccabean revolt from 168 B.C.

Pompey captures Jerusalem 63 B.C.

Romans make Herod king of Judea 37 B.C.

Augustus Caesar becomes Roman Emperor 29 B.C.

The Romans take over

The Maccabees' successors became local kings. Sadly, some of them turned out to be not much better than Antiochus.

But the Greek Empire soon collapsed, and was taken over by the Romans. An army led by Pompey marched into Jerusalem in 63 B.C., and from then on the Jewish people lived under Roman occupation.

The Romans appointed a local ruler to look after Palestine, as they did in some other countries. This ruler had a difficult job—to keep both the local people and their Roman overlords happy.

Jews and Romans

Within the Jewish nation, people reacted in different ways to being a part of the Roman Empire.

Some saw the chance to make a lot of money. They hired themselves out to the Romans as tax collectors and government officials. But they were a minority.

The Zealots were guerilla fighters, who took every chance they could to fight against the Romans. During Jesus' lifetime there were many revolts. None of them succeeded, but many Jewish fighters lost their lives.

Others knew that no one could change much. They went off to live in remote places in the deserts of Judea, and waited for God to step in to put things right.

Jewish religion

There were two influential groups in the Jewish religion at the time of Jesus.

One group was the Sadducees. They were mainly wealthy aristocrats and priests. They refused to update the old law of Moses, and as a result did not believe in life after death; and they did not expect God to intervene and to change things in any way.

The Sadducees were the most important group in the Jewish religious council that met in Jerusalem. This council was called the Sanhedrin.

The other group was the Pharisees. They included many scribes—the people who were responsible for preserving and explaining the Jewish law. The Pharisees were concerned to interpret the old law very precisely for their own lives, working out what was the "right" thing to do in every possible situation! Many local religious teachers—the rabbis—were Pharisees.

Unlike the Sadducees, the Pharisees expected God to send them a deliverer—a Messiah—who would restore their nation's power.

2 The Romans

The Romans conquered a huge empire that spread to all the countries around the Mediterranean Sea. Palestine, where Jesus lived, was just part of that empire.

◀ **A ruthless army**
Roman soldiers made sure that everyone obeyed the emperor. Legionaries in Palestine wore chain armor like this. Their officers—centurions—wore plumes on their helmets.

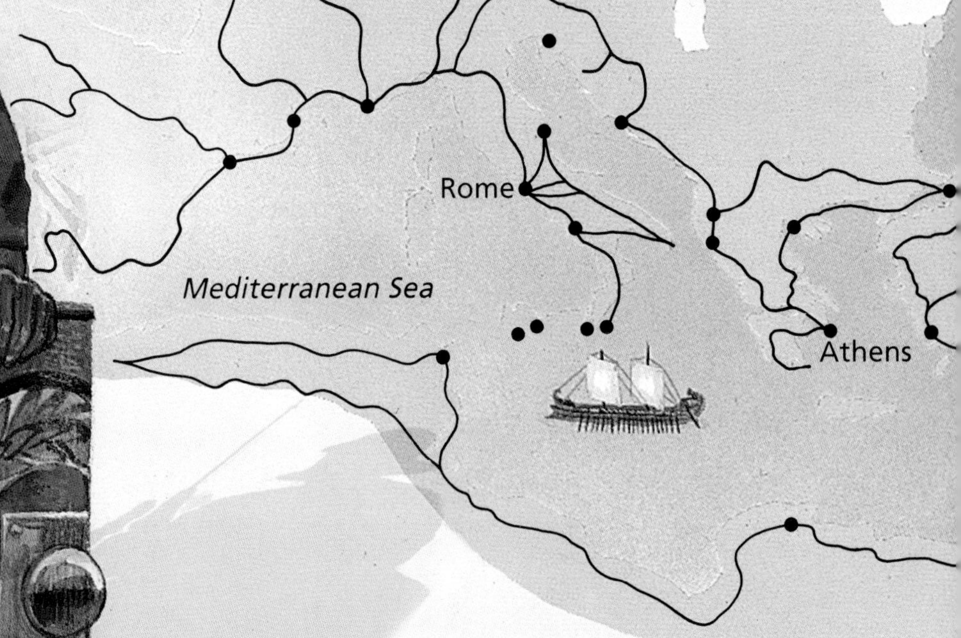

Mediterranean Sea

Rome

Athens

▶**Dealing with rebellion**
The Romans had to deal with many rebellions in Palestine. They used a stone-throwing catapult like this to capture rebellious towns. The Roman catapult balls below destroyed the synagogue in a little town called Gamla. They still lie in the ancient ruins of the building.

▼ International travel

The Romans built straight, well-paved roads, so the army could travel swiftly wherever it was needed in the empire.

Other people could travel easily too, and goods could be traded with other countries. This map shows the main roads and cities.

Jerusalem

▲ Roman worship

For the most part in the Roman Empire, people were left to worship as they wished. However, everyone in the Empire was expected to worship the Roman state gods and goddesses, such as Jupiter. And most emperors were declared gods after they died, and they had to be honored. How to honor God and the emperor was a problem for Jews and for all the followers of Jesus.

▼ Circus games

The Romans enjoyed thrilling sports such as chariot racing. Herod had a sports arena built at Caesarea in Palestine so the Roman soldiers' garrison there could watch sporting events.

3 Waiting for a King

The Jewish nation had been oppressed by other people for nearly 600 years. Now they were ruled by the Romans. Yet their Hebrew Scriptures—the special writings that form the Old Testament—had many great promises telling of their special place in the plans of God.

God's promised king

Many Old Testament passages talk about a king who would be sent by God to make the Jewish nation great again.

After their long and troubled history, the people knew that promises like these were unlikely to come true through the lives of ordinary kings. God would have to step in and send the greatest leader of all: the Messiah.

By the time of Jesus, many felt the time was right for the ancient promises to come true, and they prayed that God would save the people.

Here are some of the Scriptures that tell of God's promise to send a king who would rescue the Jewish nation.

Messiah

The word "Messiah" comes from the Hebrew word *Mashiach* and means "an anointed one." In the Old Testament both priests and kings were anointed with oil. The ceremony was simple: it consisted of pouring a little oil over their head. Nevertheless it had a very special meaning—to show that they were really being given the authority that went along with their new role, and to set them aside for the service of God. The Messiah was to serve God—and also to speak and act in God's name.

A child is born to us!
    A son is given to us!
    And he will be our ruler.
He will be called, "Wonderful Counsellor,"
    "Mighty God," "Eternal Father,"
    "Prince of Peace."
His royal power will continue to grow;
    His kingdom will always be at peace.

Bethlehem Ephrathah, you are one of the smallest towns in Judah, but out of you I will bring a ruler for Israel, whose family line goes back to ancient times.

Rejoice, rejoice, people of Zion!
    Shout for joy, you people of Jerusalem!
    Look, your king is coming to you!
...Your king will make peace among the nations;
    he will rule from sea to sea.

THE KING IS COMING

Zacharias was a priest. He and other priests shared the work of organizing the services in God's temple. He was a good man, but one thing made him sad: he and his wife Elizabeth had no children.

One day Zacharias was chosen to burn the incense on the altar in the holiest part of the temple. It was a very special day for him. Zacharias was all alone. And then God's messenger, the angel Gabriel, came to him.

"Don't be afraid, Zacharias," the angel said. "God has sent me to tell you that you and your wife Elizabeth will have a son. Call him John. He will grow up to be a great man, for God has chosen your son to tell the people that their king is coming. John will help them get ready to welcome him."

When his little son was born, Zacharias was full of joy. He remembered all God's promises in the Scriptures to rescue the Jewish people from their enemies. He declared that the time when God would do that was very near. People would be happy, as they are when day dawns after a long, dark night.

The holy place

Zacharias was burning incense on the incense altar that stood in the holy place at the center of the temple. Also there was the seven-branched lampstand, hammered out of one piece of gold; and a gold-overlaid table for the twelve loaves that were offered each Sabbath for each of the twelve tribes of Israel—the table of showbread.

A curtain screened the holy place from the Holy of holies, an inner room kept special for God that only the high priest could enter on a festival called the "Day of Atonement."

4 The Birth Day

The story of Jesus' birth is one of the best-known stories in the whole world.

Two stories about the birth day appear in the New Testament: at the beginning of Matthew's book about Jesus, and at the beginning of Luke's.

Mary and Joseph were probably teenagers. They were certainly in love, but they were not yet married. Then Mary heard that she was going to have a baby. An angel told her the news, saying that this baby would be special—God's own child. Later, Joseph also heard from the angel, and he was happy to look after Mary and provide for her as she had her baby.

THE EMPEROR'S NEW LAW

The Roman Emperor, Augustus, issued an order. Everyone in the Roman Empire must register at the town their family came from. Augustus wanted to make sure he had everyone on his list, and that they paid their taxes!

Joseph lived and worked in Nazareth. But his family was descended from King David. So he had to go to Bethlehem, where King David was born. Mary made the long journey with him although her baby was due to be born any day.

The night they arrived in Bethlehem, Mary's baby son was born. There was no room for them with the other travelers in the crowded inn, so she wrapped the baby warmly in the clothes she had made, and put him in a manger to sleep.

▶ **The journey**
The distance between Nazareth and Bethlehem is about 68 miles. Ordinary people would usually travel such a distance on foot. Some people had donkeys, which could carry one rider and quite a lot of baggage.

Shepherds and angels

When Jesus was born, some shepherds were out on the hillside above Bethlehem. They had to keep watch at night to protect their sheep from danger: wild animals, perhaps, or thieves. Those were the usual problems they had to deal with. But this night was unlike any other: they saw a terrifying sight, and a bright shining light...

It was an angel of God. "Don't be afraid," said the angel. "I am here with good news for you, which will bring great joy to all the people. This very day in David's town your Savior was born—Christ the Lord! And this is what will prove it to you: you will find the baby wrapped in swaddling clothes and lying in a manger." And suddenly a great army of heaven's angels appeared, all praising God.

The shepherds just had to go and see for themselves. Ordinary people were not usually the first to hear such special news. But when they got to the place where the manger was, it was just as the angels had told them.

Did you know?

No one really knows the date of Jesus' birth. However, it is not very likely that it was in wintertime. The shepherds were out on the hillsides the night Jesus was born, so it must have been during a warm time of year.

Christians began celebrating Jesus' birth on December 25 in 336 A.D., to replace a pagan festival in the Roman Empire.

Jesus wasn't born exactly between 1 B.C. and 1 A.D. either. The most likely year is 5 or 6 B.C.. Back in the Middle Ages someone made a mistake working out the exact date—and people have been stuck with it ever since.

◄ The baby in the manger

Mary had no cradle for her baby in the place where she was staying. She had to put Jesus in a feed trough, a manger. A typical manger could have been a hollowed-out piece of limestone like this.

Tradition says that the place where Mary and Joseph stayed may have been an animal room made in a natural cave. In this case, the manger might have been carved out of the rock wall of the cave.

5 King Herod and the Wise Men

When Jesus was born, Herod the Great was king of Judea. He was a clever man, but very brutal.

The Romans made Herod king in 37 B.C.. He tried hard to help the Jews, and started many great building projects, including a magnificent new temple in Jerusalem, great fortresses and fine new cities. But he made many enemies. The Jews disliked him because he was only half Jewish. And he was unspeakably cruel. He killed anyone who disagreed with him, even his own family. His wife Mariamne, and his sons Alexander, Aristobulus and Antipater were all put to death on his orders.

▼ The port of Caesarea

Herod's greatest city project was a massive new port on the Mediterranean Sea—Caesarea. Blocks of stone nearly 50 feet long were sunk into the water to be foundations for the wide, curving breakwaters that provided shelter for the largest Roman ships. There was also a temple to Augustus, a theater and an amphitheater.

The engineers also had to provide a water supply for the town. It came from springs on Mount Carmel, along 6 miles of tunnel and then 6 miles of aqueduct.

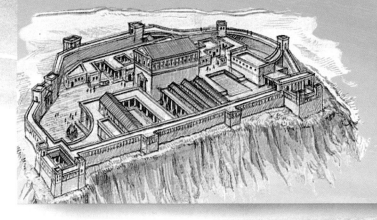

Herod's castles

Herod had gained power by using force, and he was afraid that his rivals would try to get rid of him by the same means. He built several great castles where he could live safely. They had pleasant rooms to live in, a good water supply that would be vital if the place were to be besieged, and places to house soldiers and store weapons. The aerial view shows the many buildings inside the fort of Machaerus, not far from the Dead Sea.

▲ Ancient pillars
Stone pillars from Caesarea. Long after Herod's time, they were used to build breakwaters.

Did you know?

The wise men followed a star that brought them to Bethlehem. They were probably astrologers, who made a special study of the planets. The story about them is in the book of Matthew. It does not say how many wise men there were, though tradition says there were three because they brought three gifts: gold, frankincense and myrrh.

THE WISE MEN VISIT JESUS

Wise men from the east arrived in Jerusalem. "Tell us where we can find the baby who is born to be King of the Jews," they said. "We have seen his star and come to pay him homage."

Soon all the people in Jerusalem were talking about the strangers and their question. What could it mean? Herod was most alarmed when he heard the news. He did not want a rival king in his land. He sent for the priests and teachers of God's law.

"When the Savior comes, where will he be born?" Herod asked.

"In Bethlehem," they answered, "that is what God's prophets say."

Then Herod had a secret meeting with the wise men. He wanted to find out when they first saw the star, to know how old this baby king was.

"Go to Bethlehem," he said, "and when you find the child, let me know so that I can come and pay my respects, too."

So the strangers came to Bethlehem, still following the star. They found the baby with Mary his mother. Then they brought out presents—gold, sweet-smelling frankincense and a spicy ointment called myrrh.

Babies beware!

The wise men found the baby they were looking for, but they did not tell Herod where this new King was. Instead they returned home by a different route. Herod was furious. In typical fashion, he ordered all boys in Bethlehem aged two and under to be killed.

But Jesus escaped. An angel had warned Mary and Joseph what was happening, and they left the country to go to Egypt.

6 At Home in Nazareth

Jesus grew up in the small town of Nazareth, in the region of Galilee. Mary and Joseph took him back there when he was a young boy. They had heard that King Herod had died, and felt it was safe to return from Egypt.

Nothing more is known for sure about Jesus' childhood. It is likely that he lived a very normal and ordinary life with Mary and Joseph and a group of relatives. Mark's book about Jesus talks about brothers, but the word used can also mean cousins.

Jesus' mother, Mary, continued to take a keen interest in what her son was up to all through his life. However, Joseph may well have died when Jesus was still young. His name is never mentioned after the story of Jesus' birth.

▲ Nazareth
Nazareth today, as in Jesus' time, is a busy market town for the region of Galilee.

Galilee

The region of Galilee was ruled by one of Herod's sons, Herod Antipas. Many non-Jewish ("Gentile") people lived there. Traders from all over the Empire passed through, and the main customs post at the border was just down the road at Capernaum. Not far away, the hot springs at Tiberias attracted many tourists.

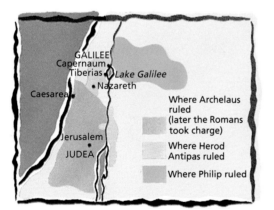

GALILEE
Capernaum
Tiberias
Lake Galilee
Nazareth
Caesarea
Jerusalem
JUDEA

Where Archelaus ruled (later the Romans took charge)

Where Herod Antipas ruled

Where Philip ruled

Did you know?

When Herod the Great died, his kingdom was divided among his three sons. Herod Antipas ruled Galilee. Another, Archelaus, ruled so badly that in 6 A.D. the emperor made his region into a Roman province that was governed by a Roman prefect. The third son, Philip, was a good ruler. He governed an area in the far north.

Work

Jesus worked in the same trade that Joseph followed—as the local builder, making all kinds of things out of wood and stone. He may have had his own small construction business.

Nazareth itself was a small place, but there were other towns and villages nearby, and Jesus would have worked throughout the region. He would often have come into contact with other young men who also had their own businesses—such as the fishermen on Lake Galilee. It was from among people like this that Jesus chose his first disciples.

Four languages

Jesus would have been familiar with four languages:

Aramaic The language that most Jews used at home, and the one that Jesus would have spoken with local people.

Greek The language most widely used all over the Roman Empire, and spoken by tourists and travelers.

Hebrew The language of the Scriptures, the Old Testament, that Jesus would have learned with other boys his age at the synagogue school.

Latin The language used for official documents in the Roman Empire.

The books about Jesus in the New Testament were written in Greek. There are just a few phrases quoting what Jesus said in Aramaic.

◀ **The work Jesus did**
This building scene shows the type of work Jesus did, making things from wood and stone.

The synagogue

The synagogue was the center of religious and community life. Every Sabbath the people gathered to pray and hear the reading of God's Law, followed by a talk from a religious teacher to help them follow their faith. Jesus would have had all his education in a synagogue school.

Whenever they could, Jewish families traveled to Jerusalem to worship in the temple. When Jesus was twelve, he went there with his family. A story in the Bible says that he stayed behind with the religious leaders to talk about God. They were amazed that someone so young had such a deep understanding of God.

7 Special Assignment

When he was almost thirty years old, Jesus was ready for the special work God had given him.

John prepares the way

By this time, Zacharias's son John had begun to announce that God's Messiah was on the way. He invited people to be baptized, as a sign that they were willing to change and live as God wants—so they would be ready to welcome the Messiah. Much to John's surprise, Jesus came and asked to be baptized in the River Jordan along with all the other people.

At Jesus' baptism, two special things happened:

▶ A dove, representing the Holy Spirit—God's presence with Jesus—came down from heaven on Jesus.

▶ God's voice said, "You are my own dear Son. I am pleased with you."

Jesus had always known he was special. Now he knew for certain that God had called him to some very important work.

Baptism
The word "baptism" comes from a Greek word meaning "to dip". John baptized people in the River Jordan.

▲ A stretch of the River Jordan in Galilee

Temptations

After his baptism, Jesus went to the Judean desert for forty days. It was a place where he could be sure of having time alone to think about his special work: to bring God's message to the people. He probably wondered what the best way to do this would be.

Maybe he could work lots of miracles to convince people he was the Messiah.

Or perhaps he could be a king with a large army and empire, just like the Romans.

Or he could do something spectacular—like throwing himself off the top of the temple in Jerusalem, knowing that God would keep him from being hurt.

But this was not God's way. Jesus knew that to serve God he would need to join with the poor and oppressed people in his nation, and share in their suffering in order to point them to God.

▲ **Rocks in the desert**
Jesus' hunger drove him to think about the value of miracles. No doubt some of the rocks in the desert even looked like the flat barley bread he longed for so much, and made him wonder if he should actually turn the stones into bread.

God's special message

The only way all the wrongs in the world will be put right, Jesus said, is if people are prepared to see things the way God sees them. His message was simple: "Change the way you look at things—and trust me."

Many people were interested—people such as Jesus' first disciples, the fishermen Peter, Andrew, James and John. "I need people like you to join me," Jesus said. "You're good at catching fish. Would you come with me and share the good news of God's love with anyone who will hear?"

They were so surprised that a religious teacher should be interested in them, they said yes right away—and began the adventure of a lifetime.

◀ **Fishermen at work**
Jesus chose some of his closest followers from among the fishermen who ran their businesses on the shores of Lake Galilee. At night, they would go out in their little sailing boats to cast their nets for fish.

Disciples

The word "disciple" means "student" or "learner." All Jewish religious teachers—called rabbis—had students. Being a disciple with one of them was a great privilege, and demanded great dedication to studying the ancient teachings.

People like the fisherman Peter just didn't have the qualifications to become that kind of disciple. But Jesus always called ordinary people to help him in his work of telling people about God.

8 A New Kind of Teacher

Jesus loved being with people, and they seemed to enjoy being with him. He never organized big meetings that people would have to be invited to attend. He met people in their homes, or in the fields, or by the Lake of Galilee. He took his message about God to the places where ordinary people went about their everyday work. That was where people needed most of all to know that God was with them, as a friend.

A teacher who can be trusted

Jesus was different from many other religious teachers:

▶ He took his message to the places where people lived and worked, instead of expecting them to come to him.

▶ He spoke so simply that anyone could understand—yet with an authority that could only come from God.

▶ He often asked people questions, and was always ready to listen to what they had to say. He genuinely cared for the feelings and opinions of other people.

▶ He was one of the people himself. He lived among them. He chose ordinary friends. He went to parties, played in the street with children—and exchanged stories around the fires at nighttime.

▶ He was happy to share his message with all sorts of people: Roman officials as well as Jews with a background like his; learned rabbis and little children; men and women; rich people and poor people.

As people listened to Jesus' teaching, they knew it was for them. He welcomed ordinary people, who knew they were not perfect. He had time for those who were not naturally religious types. And he spoke of a God who was ready to welcome those who do wrong—and to forgive them and love them.

▼ **Around Lake Galilee**
Galilee is only about 40 miles long and 25 miles wide and Jesus never traveled very far. Most of his life was spent around the northwestern shores of the lake, and his home base was in Capernaum, which was also Peter's hometown. His teaching was given to ordinary farmers and fishing people in the area around his own home.

- Caesarea Philippi
- Bethsaida
- Capernaum
- *Lake Galilee*
- Nazareth
- SAMARIA
- DECAPOLIS
- Jericho
- Jerusalem
- JUDEA

HOW TO BE HAPPY

Huge crowds flocked to see Jesus. They came from all over the country. One day, when he saw how many there were, Jesus led them up a hill. He sat down, and began to talk to them about God.

Some of the people there were poor. Some of them were hungry. They didn't count for much in the mighty Roman Empire. But as citizens of God's kingdom, they would have everything.

"Happy are you poor," Jesus said,
   "the Kingdom of God is yours!
Happy are you who are hungry now;
   you are going to be full!

Happy are you who cry now;
   you are going to laugh!
Happy are you when people hate you and reject you for being my friends. A great reward is waiting for you in heaven."

Jesus could see that some of his listeners were puzzled. So he went on:

"You are all such worriers. You worry about what you are going to eat and what you are going to wear. But there's more to life than food and clothes. Look at the birds flying overhead. God takes care of them— and God cares much more about you!"

9 New Power

From the beginning, Jesus had turned away from the temptation to work miracles for his own benefit. Yet he had special God-given power that enabled him to do many remarkable things. As well as being an interesting teacher, Jesus was also a miracle-worker. Jesus' miracles are his words in action.

Jesus and the environment

Lake Galilee often looks calm and still, but fierce storms can blow up with no warning. When Jesus calmed a storm on Lake Galilee, it showed that his message about God's coming kingdom was not just about people becoming God's friends: it would include bringing calm and order into the environment, the whole world of nature.

How did Jesus work miracles?

Jesus claimed that he had God's power to work miracles, but not everyone believed him. Some thought there must be something wrong with him, that perhaps he was under the influence of the devil.

Jesus' disciples, who saw him work many miracles, realized that he used his power for good, and not for evil. For them, there could only be one answer: that power must come from God. They saw the miracles as a sure sign that Jesus was God's special king, the Messiah.

Feeding the hungry

The Old Testament had something to say about what the Messiah would do when he came. Among other things, he would feed hungry people—and when Jesus fed more than 5,000 people from just five loaves and two fish, many people recognized him as the Messiah.

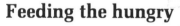

▼ Five loaves and two fish

STORM ON THE LAKE

It was a calm evening. The lake was peaceful and still as Jesus and his followers got into the boat to cross to the other side. Jesus had not had a moment to himself all day. He was very tired and soon fell asleep.

Then with no warning, a strong wind began to blow. In no time the water was whipped into angry waves. The little boat tossed. The men struggled with the oars. But Jesus slept on.

The storm grew worse. The waves broke over the sides of the boat, and it began to fill with water. The men weren't easily frightened. They were fishermen. They had seen plenty of storms in their time. But now it seemed as if nothing could save them. How could Jesus sleep through it all?

They shook him awake.

"Wake up! Wake up!" they shouted. "We're going to drown."

Jesus stood up. He spoke to the howling wind and the steep-pitched waves.

"Be still!" he commanded.

And there was calm.

Then he said to his followers: "Where is your faith?"

No one said a word. They had been afraid of the storm. Now they felt a little afraid of Jesus. He looked like any normal man. And yet the wind and waves obeyed his orders.

"Who can he really be?" they whispered to one another.

11 Jesus Shares a Secret

Everyone could see that Jesus knew God really well. He told his disciples that they too could know God in a personal way—as well as they knew their own parents.

A loving God

Powerful people can often be dangerous, using their strength to abuse others weaker than themselves. People have often thought of God like that: as powerful and dangerous, very angry, and always wanting to hurt people and make them feel useless. Jesus said the exact opposite. God is really nice, he said, and loves us even better than the most caring parent you could ever imagine.

Jesus encouraged his disciples to keep in close touch with God through prayer: talking to God, and listening too.

▼ Family love

Jesus said that human parents, for all their failings, would always try to provide good food for their children. No one would give a child a stone instead of bread, or a snake instead of a fish, or a scorpion instead of an egg.

He also said that God is like the best possible kind of parent, and wants to give people good things.

A quiet place to pray

Jesus said that people should take time alone to pray. He criticized those who stood on the street corner to pray, because they were just showing off. Jesus said that prayer should be something done quietly. He told people to go into a room and close the door when they wanted to pray. He himself took time in the early morning to go off to a quiet place out of doors, such as the hills around Lake Galilee, in order to talk to God.

The prayer Jesus taught

Jesus told his disciples to talk to God in prayer like this:

Our Father in heaven:
May your holy name be honored;
May your Kingdom come.
May your will be done on earth as it is in heaven.
Give us today the food we need.
Forgive us the wrongs we have done, as we forgive the wrongs that others have done to us.
Do not bring us to hard testing, but keep us safe from the Evil One.

▲ **Everyday needs**
Jesus said that God wants people to ask for the things they need, such as food to eat.

The very best kind of parent

Jesus called God his "Father." That doesn't mean God is a man—nor that God is like our own fathers. Not everyone gets along well with their father. Jesus was thinking of the best possible kind of parent you could imagine, and saying, "That's what God is like."

Jesus once said, "Whoever has seen me has seen the Father." That meant that God is like Jesus: wanting to spend time and effort being a friend and helper to all kinds of people, and treating every single person as special.

A practical prayer

Jesus' prayer asks for God's will to be done on earth. God cares what happens here!

It reminds people to ask God for what they need. God is interested in whether or not people have enough to eat and the other things they need to live.

It reminds people to think about their own actions. Everyone is quick to notice when someone hurts them ... but slower to see how their actions might be hurting others. God wants people to show love for one another, and to ask for forgiveness when they fail.

12 The Healer

Jesus helped people in many different ways. He spoke of God's love for those who were suffering. He showed it by making many people better.

Jesus and suffering

Jesus always had a special concern for those whom others despised. He even touched people that no one else would approach—people who suffered from leprosy, for example. This was a dreadful skin disease that was easily passed on to other people, and anyone who caught it was chased out of their home to live as best they could in the countryside.

Getting through to Jesus

One day Jesus was teaching inside a house. The place was so full that no one could even get near the door. But four men came along carrying their friend, who was unable to walk. He was on the thin mattress that served as a bed.

When the men saw the crowd, they went up the outside staircase and onto the roof. That was ordinary enough. But they had a plan that was quite out of the ordinary!

The clay surface of the roof was not particularly strong ... anyone with a bit of determination could break it up quite easily. And that's what they did—until they had dug a hole through the middle of the roof. Then they lowered the man down to where Jesus was.

THE MAN IN THE GRAVEYARD

On the shore of the Lake of Galilee, just across from his home town, Jesus met a man who was really insane. People were so afraid of him they tried to chain him up in a graveyard. As Jesus approached, he could see why they did that. The man was shouting and screaming, flinging himself to the ground and injuring himself with stones and knives. He had no idea who he really was—he seemed to have been taken over by thousands of different personalities.

Jesus felt really sorry for him. "Come out of this man," Jesus ordered, so that he could be himself. There was a great commotion, as what seemed like thousands of demons were let loose. But in no time at all, the man was well. He sat and talked with Jesus—and then went off to tell his family what a difference Jesus had brought into his life.

Jesus was certainly surprised to see him. But it was obvious that the men all trusted him and believed he could give the sick man his strength back again.

That is exactly what Jesus did.

"Stand up, and carry your bed back home!" he instructed. To everyone's amazement, the man did just that.

◀ **A hole in the roof**
It was easy to make a sizeable hole in the roof by breaking up the clay surface and pulling aside the network of branches on top of the beams.

People Jesus healed

Jesus healed people with particular diseases, such as leprosy. He gave strength to people's limbs, made deaf people hear again, and gave sight to the blind.

He freed people who were troubled by evil spirits. He often said that God wanted to release people from the power of evil. In these miracles, he proved it.

Other people suffered from mental illness: Jesus made them well again.

Death frightens us all. The daughter of a man named Jairus, a widow's son, Jesus' friend Lazarus—they were all brought to life again. Those who saw these miracles had a glimpse of what was to come later, when Jesus himself returned from the grave.

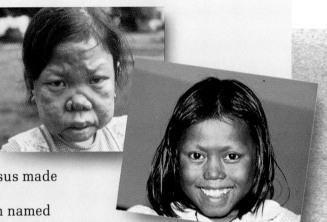

▲ **Healing**
Life is so much better if you are well. Think how much this little girl's life improved when doctors healed her leprosy. Jesus healed people in even more dramatic ways.

◀ **A great commotion**
The story in Mark's book says that the destructive powers that had tormented the man went into a herd of pigs, which then went rushing madly into the lake.

Everyone who met him could see that Jesus must be someone special. But just who was he?

John the Baptist's question

John the Baptist was one of the first to recognize that Jesus must be the promised Messiah. Like everyone else, John expected him to be a soldier. If the Messiah had come to deliver people, then there was only one thing they needed saving from: the Romans who had occupied their land. But Jesus never formed an army. He actually told people to love their enemies.

John was arrested and thrown into prison for criticizing the king, Herod Antipas. Afterwards, he sent his disciples to Jesus with a question.

"Tell us," they asked, "are you the one John said was going to come, or should we expect someone else?"

Jesus pointed to all the remarkable things that were happening because of him: "The blind can see, the lame can walk, those who suffer from leprosy are made clean, the deaf hear, the dead are brought back to life, and the Good News is preached to the poor." These were all things God had promised would happen when the Messiah came.

The disciples wonder

Even the disciples had questions about who Jesus was. One day, Jesus asked Peter who people thought he was. Peter replied that some said Jesus was a great prophet and a great teacher.

"But who do *you* say I am?" Jesus asked. And Peter gave his answer:

"You are the Messiah, the Son of the living God."

Just after this, Jesus went to a mountain to pray. He took three disciples who were especially close to him: Peter, James and John. As they watched, a remarkable change came over Jesus. His face and his clothes became dazzlingly bright. And a voice spoke: "This is my own dear Son, with whom I am pleased—listen to him."

"I Am..."

John was one of the disciples, and he wrote a book about Jesus. In his book he recorded seven sayings describing Jesus.

▼

▼ Bread
One of Jesus' miracles was to feed thousands of people with just a few loaves. But Jesus said that he had more to offer than bread for the stomach. He said:
"I am the bread of life, and whoever comes to me will never be hungry."

◄ Light
In Jesus' day people used oil lamps like this to light their homes. Jesus said:
"I am the light of the world, and whoever follows me will have the light of life and will never walk in darkness."

◄ Vine
Grapevines were common in Jesus' country. Weak branches are pruned off and die. The good branches that are left flourish and produce fruit. Jesus said:
"I am the vine, and you are the branches."

The Messiah's aim

Even when the disciples believed that Jesus was the Messiah, one thing still puzzled them. Why did he not do what they expected their Messiah to do—gather an army and fight the Romans? Everybody hated the Romans and wanted to see them defeated. How could somebody as powerless as Jesus be a truly important person?

The disciples still had to learn an important lesson. It is not strong, violent people who are valued by God, but those who are weak and powerless. Jesus told them they must become like children to follow him, but they found it hard to understand what that meant.

◀ Life
When a friend of Jesus named Lazarus died, Jesus brought him to life again. It was a sign of God's power over death. Jesus said:
"I am the resurrection and the life. Whoever believes in me will live, even though they die."

▼ Shepherd
Shepherds in Jesus' day took care of their sheep day and night, finding them pasture and protecting them from danger. Jesus said:
"I am the good shepherd, who is willing to die for the sheep."

▶ Gate
This traditional sheepfold is a low enclosure with just one entrance where sheep can come in and be kept safe. Jesus said:
"I am the gate for the sheep. Whoever comes in by me will be saved."

▲ Path
A path shows the traveler the way to go. People asked Jesus how they could find God. Jesus said:
"I am the way, the truth, and the life."

14 The Good News

Crowds followed Jesus wherever he went. "If this is what God's kingdom is like," they said, "then we all want to be a part of it!"

Following Jesus

Religious teachers sometimes lay down lots of religious rules. Jesus' message was quite different. "Come and follow me," he said.

Peter had been by his fishing boat when he heard that invitation, but he went with Jesus right away. It was like the start of a great journey of discovery. In the months that followed, Peter learned lots of new things—about Jesus and about himself. Many times Peter had to change the way he thought and the way he behaved. It could be hard to follow Jesus because he was so good.

But Peter knew it was worth the effort. The one thing he especially liked was the way Jesus listened to what other people were saying. Jesus always accepted people the way they were and then invited them to follow him. He didn't mind if people had questions. In fact, Jesus was always asking questions himself, and then telling stories to help people understand what loving God was really like.

◀ **Life-giving water**
Green plants flourish beside a watercourse in Israel, but all around is dry desert. Jesus' listeners might have remembered a scene such as this when he spoke about life-giving water.

People Jesus met

Jesus always chose his words with care so that people could understand his message.

One day he met a woman by a well. She was there to draw water and take it back to the village for her family. Jesus spoke with her about water. "This isn't the only kind of water there is," he said. "I can give you water that will refresh your spirit, and help you to know God." This was just what the woman wanted to hear—and she went off home to tell all her friends about Jesus.

One night, a Pharisee called Nicodemus sent for Jesus. "What you really need," said Jesus, "is to be born anew." That sounded very strange: how could anyone possibly be born a second time? Jesus explained that to follow him a person needs to see things in a different way—the way that God sees things. Nicodemus got the message—that people are naturally interested in themselves above all. But Jesus was telling him that God wants people to put two things first: "Love the Lord your God with all your heart, with all your soul, with all your mind, and with all your strength. And love other people the way you love yourself."

▼ A new life
Jesus told a grown-up, Nicodemus, that those who want to follow him must be born again.

Another time, Jesus was talking with a rich man. "Before you can be my disciple, you should sell everything you have," Jesus told him. That was really bad news for the rich man. He wanted to love God, but he also loved his money. "No one can serve two masters," said Jesus, "and you can't love God and money at the same time." The man knew he would need to live in a different way to follow Jesus, and he was sad about what Jesus said.

◀ Treasure
Coins used in Palestine in the first century.

15 Friends and Enemies

There were thousands of people who loved listening to Jesus. But not everyone liked him. Before long, some were plotting ways they could get rid of him.

Jesus and his friends

Jesus made friends easily. He liked going to parties and visiting homes. He was the sort of person everyone wanted to know, and he was happy to be with anyone who would take his message seriously.

Jewish religious teachers at the time of Jesus had strict rules about the sort of people with whom they should mix. A Jewish rabbi once said that talking with children and spending time with people who were not well educated would prevent a person getting to know God. Jesus was not like that at all.

When his disciples were arguing about which of them would be the greatest, Jesus told them they needed to be like children or they could never be a part of God's kingdom.

He welcomed women who wanted to discuss his message with him—something no other religious teacher of his day would have allowed.

He healed people whom no one else would deal with. He even touched people suffering from leprosy, who had been driven away from their homes because people were afraid of their disease.

Enemies

It's not surprising that Jesus made enemies of the religious leaders of his day. Many of his followers were people they would disapprove of—poor people, children, women and foreigners.

He refused to keep many of the religious laws. He healed people on the weekly holy

Children
Jesus told his disciples that children are very important to God. Grown-ups need to learn from children if they want to be part of God's kingdom.

day (the Sabbath) and ignored other religious rules, too.

He claimed to be able to do things only God can do, such as forgiving sins. His disciples believed he could, because he was God's Son, but many religious leaders couldn't accept that.

By the time Jesus made his final trip to Jerusalem, many Jewish leaders had already decided to have him killed there.

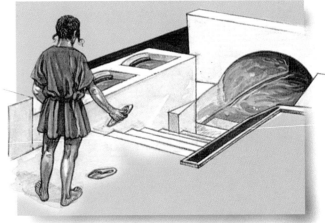

▶ **Rules about washing**
The religious people of Jesus' day had very strict rules about washing, and the wealthier people had special baths in their homes. They did not like Jesus saying that washing did not make them clean in God's eyes.

THE ANGRY CROWD

One day as Jesus was teaching, some religious leaders dragged a woman up to him. "This woman was caught having an affair with a man who is not her husband," they said. Now this was a very serious thing and the religious laws demanded that she should be taken and put to death by having huge stones thrown at her. "What do you think we should do?" they asked Jesus.

At first Jesus said nothing. He just bent down and wrote something in the dust of the ground. Then he looked at them all and said, "If any of you has never done any wrong, then that person can throw the first stone at this woman."

They all knew this was impossible, for they had all broken God's laws at some time. So they left, one by one, until only Jesus and the woman were there. "Well," said Jesus, "it seems there's no one left to punish you—and I'm certainly not going to do it. But make sure you don't break God's laws again."

16 The Triumphant King

Jesus felt most at home in Galilee. That was where he grew up, and where most of his friends lived. But the capital of the Jewish nation was Jerusalem. The temple was there, and the Jewish ruling council, the Sanhedrin, met there. And that was where Jesus finally had to take his message.

Jerusalem

Jesus visited Jerusalem on many occasions. He went there for the last time along with great crowds who were going to celebrate the annual festival of Passover. As he stood on a hilltop looking out over the city, he wept when he realized how much he really loved its people, and yet how unwilling they were to listen to his teaching. Sadly, Jesus said, "How often I wanted to gather your children together, the way a hen gathers her chickens under her wings—but you would not have it."

Over many centuries, God had sent messengers to this place, bringing good news of love and blessing. Most of the messengers had been beaten up, even killed. That is what had happened to some of the great prophets—and as Jesus went to Jerusalem, he could sense that this was what would happen to him.

Yet, even in Jerusalem, some people were eager to listen to Jesus. They knew he was really the Messiah, and were glad to welcome him to their city.

▲ **A view of Jerusalem**
When Jesus came to Jerusalem for the last time, he stayed in Bethany. Travelers approaching from that direction come around the shoulder of the Mount of Olives, and the city is spread before them, across the valley.

GOD'S KING

As soon as people knew Jesus was coming into Jerusalem, they went out to meet him. Jesus was riding a donkey, and some of the people spread their coats on the road before him. Others cut branches from palm trees to wave.

So Jesus rode into the city like a king—but one who enters in peace. "Here comes God's king," they shouted. "Praise God!"

He went to the temple. When he saw people selling animals and changing money, he was very angry. "God's temple should be a place for prayer," he said, "not a place for making money." Then he overturned the dealers' tables and drove them out.

Jesus' enemies knew now that they must get rid of him.

Did you know?

Pilgrims came from all over the Empire to worship at the temple. They needed to change their money for local coins—including the silver they needed to pay the temple tax. They also needed to buy a pigeon or other animal to offer as a sacrifice.

Jesus' week in Jerusalem

During his last week in Jerusalem, Jesus visited the temple, telling the people what it really means to worship God. "You can worship God anywhere," he said, "even without a splendid building like this."

He spoke of the end of the world. "At that time, all the wrong in the world will be put right," he told his disciples, "and God's kingdom will bring love and justice to everyone."

He stayed in the nearby village of Bethany with his friends Mary and Martha, and spent much time encouraging them to trust in God.

But all the time, he knew that others were plotting to get rid of him.

◀ The temple courtyard

People from all nations were allowed to enter the vast courtyard that surrounded the temple built by Herod. The moneychangers and people selling animals would probably have set up their stalls in the colonnade, where they would get some shade from the fierce sun.

Betrayed

Jesus spent the last night of his life sharing a meal with his special friends, the disciples. Sadly, it was just a short time before one of them betrayed him to his enemies.

At that meal Jesus also showed his disciples how they should treat one another and how they should remember him.

Sharing bread and wine

Jesus took the bread and wine that were on the table ready for the Passover celebration. They were part of this special meal that was eaten only once a year. It reminded the Jewish people of how God had rescued their ancestors from slavery many centuries before.

But Jesus did something different as he took the bread in his hands. "God is still at work in the world caring for people who suffer," he said. "This is my body. Soon, I will be broken, just like this loaf. I will die—but I will be dying for you."

THE TRAITOR

When the time to celebrate the Passover meal had come, Jesus gave instructions to his disciples. "Go into the city," he said. "You'll see a man carrying a water jar. Follow him to his house. It has a room upstairs where we can have our Passover meal together."

Later, as they sat down, Jesus took a towel, poured some water into a basin, and started washing the disciples' feet. This was a servant's job, and Peter was shocked. But Jesus explained, "You must be willing to serve one another, just as I have served you."

As they shared bread and wine, they could see that Jesus was feeling sad. "One of you is going to betray me," he said. They were stunned. Only Judas knew he was the one. Jesus' enemies had offered him thirty pieces of silver for information about where Jesus was. A short while later, Judas left the other disciples to go and tell Jesus' enemies where to find him.

He poured the wine out and passed it around in a cup for them to share. "This is my blood," he said, "the sign of a new peace that God is bringing into the world."

Today, Christians all over the world still share bread and wine. This is the Mass or Eucharist, sometimes also called Holy Communion or the Lord's Supper. It reminds them of Jesus' great love for all people, and it celebrates the fact that those who follow Jesus can have peace, joy, love and forgiveness in their own lives today.

▲ **Bread and wine**
Christians today might share a loaf and cup of wine like this to remember what Jesus did.

Prayer—and arrest

After supper, Jesus took the disciples to a garden called Gethsemane. By this time Jesus was feeling very sad and very afraid. He knelt by himself to pray. "Father, if it's possible," he said, "save me from death."

But the sound of angry voices filled the garden. Jesus' enemies had brought the temple soldiers, and they were determined to arrest him. Judas, a disciple who had left the meal, was with them. In fact, he was their leader. "Arrest the man I kiss," he told the soldiers. He kissed Jesus. The soldiers grabbed Jesus roughly, and every one of his other friends ran away and left him to his fate.

▲ **Gethsemane**
Jesus went to Gethsemane because it was a quiet place to pray. But in this lonely olive orchard it was easy for his enemies to arrest him.

18 A Day of Darkness

After being arrested, Jesus was put on trial for his life. But there was no way of escape. He was brutally beaten, condemned to death, and then nailed to a cross and left to die.

Trial

From the Garden of Gethsemane, Jesus was taken to the home of Caiaphas, the high priest. "Are you the Messiah?" the high priest asked him. "Yes," replied Jesus.

The Jewish leaders simply couldn't believe this. How could someone like Jesus really be God's special messenger? Kings were supposed to be rich and powerful. Jesus was neither. The high priest was horrified, and tore his clothes to show his anger. Jesus' friends could have spoken up for him. But they had run away.

Next, Jesus was taken to Pontius Pilate, the Roman governor. 'This man claims to be king of the Jews," his enemies said. Now that was correct in a way—Jesus was certainly claiming to be the Messiah—but he was not a soldier who would fight the Romans. He called people into God's kingdom, which is concerned with love and trust and forgiveness, not with hatred and violence. Pilate seems almost to have believed him. But in the end he was not sure that Jesus wasn't a threat to law and order, so he condemned Jesus to die by being nailed to a cross.

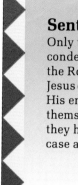

Sentence of death

Only the Romans could condemn someone to death in the Roman Empire. That is why Jesus came before Pontius Pilate. His enemies tried him themselves first, to make sure they had put together a good case against him.

Pilate's monument

This battered stone monument found in the ruins of Caesarea names Pontius Pilate as "prefect"—a title for a Roman governor. You can still see parts of the Latin words: Pontius Pilatus Praefectus.

THE KING OF THE JEWS

▲ Golgotha
Some people believe that this rocky hill resembling a skull is Golgotha, the place where Jesus was put to death.

 On a hill outside the city walls, the Roman soldiers nailed Jesus' hands and feet to the cross. The soldiers put up a notice, "This is Jesus, the king of the Jews."

The hot sun beat down, and Jesus hung there in great pain. Yet he still loved them. "Forgive them, Father," he prayed. "They don't know what they are doing."

At midday, it suddenly became dark. "O God, why have you left me?" Jesus cried. Then he gave a great shout—"It is finished"—and died.

A man called Joseph, from Arimathaea—a follower of Jesus—went to Pilate and asked if he could take Jesus' body away for burial. Pilate agreed. Joseph wrapped the body in long strips of cloth, with myrrh and other spices.

Mary Magdalene and the other women who had followed Jesus from Galilee went with Joseph and saw him put the body in a new grave, a large cave dug out of rock. A heavy stone was rolled across the entrance.

The Jewish authorities asked Pilate for a guard. They put a seal on the stone. And the guards settled down to keep watch.

Crucifixion

Crucifixion was a horrible way to die. The Roman soldiers first made cruel fun of their prisoner. They made him wear a crown of thorny stems, and jeered at the claim that he was a king. And they beat him with a scourge—a whip with sharp bones knotted among its thongs. But the crucifixion was far more dreadful. The Romans invented this method as a way of killing the worst criminals in their empire. It was very painful, and a person nailed to a cross could take many hours—sometimes days—to die. Yet to Christians, the cross is very special. For by suffering and dying there, Jesus overcame all the powers of evil, and showed just how much God loves people.

19 Alive Again!

Jesus' friends were brokenhearted when they saw Jesus die. They had expected him to change the world with his teaching about God. But what could they do now? Within three days they had the most amazing answer to their questions.

EARLY IN THE MORNING

Joseph had been in a hurry when he buried Jesus. It was a Friday afternoon, and the Jewish holy day, the Sabbath, began at sunset. No one could handle a dead body then. But early on Sunday morning, when the Sabbath was over, some of the women who followed Jesus went to the grave with spices to put on the body for a proper burial.

When they got to the tomb, they saw that the big stone had been rolled to one side. What could have happened?

Inside, to their alarm, was the shining figure of an angel. "Don't be afraid," the angel said, "I know you are looking for Jesus. But he's not here. He's alive from the dead. Look, this is where his body was—it's just an empty space now. Go quickly and tell his disciples they will see him again soon."

The women did just as the angel said. But the men couldn't believe their exciting news. Peter and John went to see for themselves.

John ran faster than Peter, and got to the tomb first. He looked inside the grave, but didn't go in. Then Peter arrived, and they both went in. The cloths which had been wrapped around the body were still in place—but empty. The men knew right away that no one could possibly have stolen the body. The women's story must be right after all—Jesus really was alive from the dead!

The men went home. But Mary Magdalene stayed there, crying. She still could not understand what had happened. Then she saw a man she thought was the gardener.

"If you have taken him away," she began, "please tell me where to find him."

The man turned towards her and spoke.

"Mary," he said—and at once she knew it was Jesus. She was filled with joy.

"Tell my friends you have seen me," Jesus said.

▼ A stone ossuary from the time of Jesus

Did you know?

Jesus' tomb was a cave with a stone rolled over its entrance. The body would be laid on a simple stone shelf, and normally left there until only the bones remained. Then—maybe a year later—the bones would be gathered together and placed in a smaller casket called an "ossuary." The tomb could then be used for another body.

Jesus is alive!

Many people wonder if Jesus really did rise from the dead. But there is no other convincing explanation of the facts.

His enemies may have taken the body. But they would surely have produced it later, to disprove the disciples' claim that Jesus was alive. That means neither Jews nor Romans took it.

Tombs were sometimes robbed by gangs of thieves looking for gold and jewelry that had been buried with the dead person. But Jesus was not rich, and grave robbers would have known that, when he was crucified, the little he had was shared out among the soldiers.

The disciples would not have taken Jesus' body themselves. They were too distressed. And later, they were ready to suffer— even to die themselves—for their belief that Jesus was alive.

None of them expected this "resurrection," as it is called. But when Jesus began to appear to them at different times and in different places, they knew it must be true.

Jesus explained how his death and resurrection were part of God's wonderful plan. He spoke about the ancient Scriptures. "God's king had to suffer and die," he said, "and live again. Death has been conquered, and the power of evil is defeated. This is good news for people of every nation—and you will go and tell them about it."

People who saw Jesus

The same day that the women claimed that Jesus was alive, he appeared to ten of the disciples in a locked room. One of the disciples, Thomas, was not there, and he didn't believe their story.

A week later, the same thing happened when Thomas was there. Jesus invited Thomas to touch the marks of the wounds in his hands and side. Thomas was convinced.

There were others, too: Cleopas and his wife talked with Jesus as they walked home to Emmaus, a village not far from Jerusalem.

Jesus' brother James became a disciple as a result of meeting the risen Jesus, and on one occasion, over five hundred of Jesus' followers all saw him at the same time.

▲ **A stone tomb**
This stone cave tomb, with its rolling stone set in a groove just beyond the covered entrance, follows the style of Herod's tomb, which can still be seen today.

20 An End and a Beginning

Jesus continued appearing to his disciples for forty days. During this special time he taught them that from now on, they would be the ones to take his teaching to other people throughout the world.

Peter's denial

When Jesus was arrested, the disciples had all run away. Peter had followed and watched from a distance while Jesus was on trial at the high priest's house. There a servant girl had asked Peter if he was one of Jesus' friends. Peter was so afraid that he said he had never met Jesus before, and got angry with the servant who asked him. Ever since, he had been struggling with his own feelings about Jesus. Was he really the Messiah? And did Peter really want to follow him? Jesus gave Peter the chance to put things right.

▼ **Before the dawn**
Before Jesus was arrested, Peter had insisted that he would never abandon him. Jesus warned him that he would do so before the cock crowed to signal the beginning of the following day.

And that is what happened: Peter followed Jesus at a distance, but when questioned by the servants at the high priest's house, he swore that he was not one of the disciples.

The third time he denied it, he heard the cock crowing.

PETER MAKES GOOD

"I'm going fishing," Peter said. His friends went with him. They worked hard all night, but caught nothing at all. As dawn broke, they were coming back. Someone standing on the shore called out to them, "Have you caught any fish?" "Nothing," they said. "Throw the net out now, and you'll make a catch." They did—and caught so many fish they could hardly pull them in.

John knew this could only be Jesus. "Bring some of the fish you've just caught," Jesus said, "and we'll make breakfast." After the meal, Jesus had a question for Peter. "Do you love me?" he asked.

"Yes," Peter replied, "you know I love you." Jesus asked the same question three times, and three times Peter gave the same answer. "Then take good care of my followers," Jesus said.

Farewells

One day Jesus met his disciples for the last time. "From now on, you will be the ones to teach people about God's kingdom," he said. "You will not always know the answers to the questions people ask you, and you will often be persecuted, thrown into jail, and even put to death for being my followers. You are just ordinary people, and God knows that. But with the power of God's Spirit you will be able to do extraordinary things."

Then Jesus disappeared—this time for good. An angel appeared and told the disciples that they would never see Jesus again. Well, not *never*, for the angel promised that in the future Jesus will return to the earth. But until that happens, his followers should take the good news of God's love and forgiveness to the whole earth.

As the disciples shared their good news, they found many people ready to listen. Soon, there were groups of Jesus' followers in towns and cities throughout the whole Roman Empire.

Today, people of all ages and in every country are fascinated by the story of this remarkable person. The child who was born in Bethlehem really has changed the world.

Jerusalem

▶News for the world
The news of God's love and forgiveness spread from the tiny band of Jesus' followers in Jerusalem to every part of the Roman Empire (shown in green) and beyond. In our time the news has spread to millions of people in every country of the world.

Finding Out More

If you want to know more about what you've read in *The Life that Changed the World*, you can look up the stories in the Bible.

The usual shorthand method has been used to refer to Bible passages. Each Bible book is split into chapters and verses. Take **Mark 1:15–17**, for example. This refers to the Gospel of Mark; chapter 1; verses 15–17.

When a reference to a Gospel story has other references after it in brackets, this means that the same story has been told by more than one of the Gospel writers.

1 The Time Before Jesus

Matthew 9:9 (Mark 2:13–17; Luke 5:27–32);
Matthew 10:4 (Mark 3:18; Luke 6:15)
    Jews and Romans

Matthew 22:22–33 (Mark 12:18–27; Luke 20:27–38);
Matthew 23:1–36 (Mark 12:38–40;
Luke 11:37–53)   **Jewish religion**

3 Waiting for a King

Genesis 15:1–7; Isaiah 32:1; Ezekiel 37:24

Isaiah 9:6–7

Micah 5:2

Zechariah 9:9–10

Exodus 30:30; 1 Samuel 10:1
    Messiah

Luke chapters 1–2 1 Kings chapter 6
    The king is coming

4 The Birth Day

Luke 2:1–7	**The emperor's new law**
Luke 2:8–20	**Shepherds and angels**
Luke 1:6–38; Matthew 1:18–24	
	Joseph and Mary

5 King Herod and the Wise Men

Matthew 2:1–12	**The wise men visit Jesus**
Matthew 2:13–18	**Babies beware!**

6 At Home in Nazareth

Luke 2:41–50	**The synagogue**

7 Special Assignment

Luke 3:7–14, 21–22	**John prepares the way**
Luke 4:1–13	**Temptations**
Mark 1:14–19	**God's special message**

8 A New Kind of Teacher

Matthew 5:1–12; 6:25–27	**How to be happy**
Matthew 6:28–30	**Wild flowers**

9 New Power

Isaiah 55:1–5; John 6:1–13	**Feeding the hungry**
Matthew 8:23–27	**Storm on the lake**
Matthew 12:22–24	**How did Jesus work miracles?**

10 The New Kingdom

Matthew 13:47–50; John 4:1–42;	
Matthew 13:24–30; 20:1–16	**Parables**
Luke 10:30–37	**The kind stranger**
Matthew 13:45–46	**An expensive pearl**
Matthew 13:1–9	**Seeds and soil**

11 Jesus Shares a Secret

Luke 11:11–13;	
Matthew 6:31–33	**Family meals**
Matthew 6:5–8; Mark 1:35	**Private prayer**
Matthew 6:9–13	**The prayer Jesus taught**
John 14:9	**The very best kind of parent**

12 The Healer

Luke 17:11–19	**Jesus and suffering**
Mark 2:3–12 (Matthew 9:2–7; Luke 5:18–25)	
	Getting through to Jesus
Mark 5:1–20 (Matthew 8:28–34; Luke 8:27–35)	
	The man in the graveyard

Matthew 12:10–13 (Mark 3:1–5; Luke 6:6–10);
Mark 7:31–37; Matthew 20:29–34; Luke 8:2;
Mark 5:22–24, 38–42 (Matthew 9:18–19, 23–25;
Luke 8:41–42, 49–56); Luke 7:11–15; John 11:1–44
People Jesus healed

13 Who Was This Man?

Matthew 11:2–6 (Luke 7:18–23)
John the Baptist's question

Matthew 16:13–16 (Mark 8:27–30; Luke 9:18–21);
Matthew 17:1–5 (Mark 9:2–13; Luke 9:28–36,
The disciples wonder

Matthew 18:1–5 (Mark 9:33–37; Luke 9:46–48)
The Messiah's aim

"I Am…"

John 6:35	**Bread**
John 8:12	**Light**
John 10:7	**Gate**
John 10:11	**Shepherd**
John 11:25	**Life**
John 14:6	**Path**
John 15:5	**Vine**

14 The Good News

Mark 1:16–18 (Matthew 4:18–20; Luke 5:9–10);
Matthew 16:21–23 (Mark 8:31–33)
Following Jesus

John 4:7–30; Matthew 19:16–22 (Mark 10:17–31;
Luke 18:18–30); Matthew 6:24 (Luke 16:13); John 3:1–8;
Mark 12:28–31 (Matthew 22:34–40; Luke 10:25–28)
People Jesus met

15 Friends and Enemies

Matthew 11:19 (Luke 7:34); Mark 2:16 (Matthew 9:10;
Luke 5:29); Mark 9:33–37 (Matthew 18:1–5;
Luke 9:46–48); Luke 10:38–41 (John 4); Luke 17:11–19
Jesus and his friends

Luke 5:33–35; Luke 6:1–5 (Matthew 12:1–8;
Mark 2:23–28); Luke 13:10–13; Mark 2:1–12
(Matthew 9:1–8; Luke 5:17–26); Matthew 16:16
(Mark 9:29; Luke 9:20); Mark 11:18
Enemies

John 8:1–11
The angry crowd

16 The Triumphant King

Matthew 20:17 (Luke 18:31; Mark 10:32); Luke 19:41;
Matthew 23:27; Mark 10:33–34; Matthew 20:18–19;
Luke 18:32–34
Jerusalem

Mark 11:7–10 (Matthew 21:8–11; Luke 19:37–40;
John 12:12–15); Matthew 21:12–17 (Mark 11:15–19;
Luke 19:45–46); Luke 19:47–48
Palm Sunday

John 4:19–24; Mark 13:13, 27; John 12:2–8
Jesus' week in Jerusalem

17 Betrayed

Exodus 12; 1 Corinthians 11:23–25
Sharing bread and wine

Luke 22:7–13 (Matthew 26:17–25; Mark 14:12–21;
John 13:21–30); John 13:1–39
The traitor

Matthew 26:36–56 (Mark 14:43–50; Luke 22:39–53;
John 18:3–12) **Prayer—and arrest**

18 A Day of Darkness

Mark 14:53–65 (Matthew 26:57–68;
Luke 22;54–55, 63–71; John 18:13–14, 19–24);
Luke 23:1–24 (Matthew 27:1–2, 11–14; Mark 15:1–5;
John 18:28–38) **Trial**

Matthew 27:32–44, 57–61 (Mark 15:21–32, 42–47;
Luke 23:26–49, 50–56; John 19:17–27, 38–42)
The king of the Jews

19 Alive Again!

Matthew 28:1–10 (Mark 16:1–8; Luke 24:1–12;
John 20:1–10) **Early in the morning**

Luke 24:44–48; Matthew 28:18–20
(Mark 16:15) **Jesus is alive!**

John 20:19–29; Luke 24:13–32 (Mark 16:12–13);
1 Corinthians 15:6, 7 **People who saw Jesus**

20 An End and a Beginning

Matthew 26:69–75 (Mark 14:66–72; Luke 22:56–62;
John 18:15–18, 25–27) **Peter's denial**

John 21:2–17 **Peter makes good**

Matthew 24:3–14; Mark 13:3–13; Luke 21:7–19;
Acts 1:9–11 **Farewells**

Index

A

Alexander the Great   1
Alexander   5
altar   3
Andrew   7
angel   3, 4, 5, 19
anointed   3
Antiochus IV   1
Antipater   5
Aramaic   6
Archelaus   6
Arimathea   18
Aristobulus   5
armor   2
army   1, 2, 7, 13
arrest   17, 18
astrologer   5
Athens   1, 2
Atonement, Day of   3
Augustus Caesar   1, 4, 5

B

Baptist, John the   3, 7, 13
baptize, baptism   7
Bethany   16
Bethlehem   3, 4, 5, 20
Bethsaida   8
blind   12, 13
bread   7, 9, 11, 13, 17
builder   6

C

Caesar, Augustus   1, 4, 5
Caesarea   2, 5, 18
Caesarea Philippi   8
Caiaphas   18
Capernaum   8
Carmel, Mount   5
carpenter see builder
catapult   2
centurion   2
chariot   2
child, children   13, 14, 15
Christ   4
Christmas   4
circus   2
cock   20
cradle   4
cross   18
crown of thorns   18
crucifixion   18

D

David, King   4
deaf   12
death   12, 13, 18, 19
Decapolis   8
devil   9
disciple   7, 11, 19

E

Egypt   1, 5
Elizabeth   3
Emmaus   19
emperor   1, 2, 4, 5
empire   1, 2, 7
environment   9
Eucharist   17

F

festival   3
fishermen   6, 7, 9, 10
forgiveness   11, 17, 18, 20
fort   5
frankincense   5
freedom fighter   1
   see also Zealots

G

Gabriel   3
Galilee, Lake   6, 7, 8, 9, 11, 12
Galilee   6, 16
Gamla   2
gate   13
Gethsemane   17
god, gods, goddess, goddesses   2
gold   3, 5
Golgotha   18
Gospel   5
Greece   1
Greek Empire   1
Greek   6

H

healing   12
heaven   8
Hebrew   3, 6
helmet   2
Herod Antipas   6, 13
Herod the Great   1, 2, 5, 6, 19
High Priest   3, 20
Holy Communion   17
Holy of holies   3
Holy Spirit   7, 20
hungry   8, 9, 11

I

incense   3
India   1

J

Jairus   12
James (brother of Jesus)   11
James (disciple)   7, 13
Jericho   8, 10
Jerusalem   1, 2, 5, 6, 7, 8, 10, 15, 16
John (disciple)   7, 13, 20
John (the Baptist)   3, 7, 13
Jordan, River   7
Joseph (husband of Mary)   4, 6
Joseph (of Arimathea)   18, 19
Judah   3
Judas (Iscariot)   17
Judas Maccabeus   1
Judea   1, 2, 5, 7, 8
Jupiter   2

K

King David   4
kingdom (God's)   3, 8, 10, 11, 14, 15, 16, 18
king   1, 3, 5, 16, 18, 19

L

lame   13
lampstand   3
Last Supper   17
Latin   6
law   1, 5, 6, 10, 15
Lazarus   12
legionary   2
leprosy   11, 13
life   12, 13, 14, 19
light   13
Lord's prayer   11
Luke   3

M

Maccabees   1
Maccabeus, Judas   1
Machaerus   5
manger   4
Mariamne   5
Mark   6, 12
Martha (sister of Mary)   16
Mary (Magdalene)   18, 19
Mary (mother of Jesus)   4, 5, 6
Mary (sister of Martha)   16
Mass   17
Matthew   4, 5
Mediterranean Sea   1, 2, 5
Messiah   1, 3, 7, 9, 13, 16, 18, 19
miracle   7, 9, 12
Mount of Olives   16
myrrh   5

N

Nazareth   4, 6, 8
New Testament   6
Nicodemus   14

O

Old Testament   3, 6, 9
ossuary   19

P

Palestine   1, 2
palm   16
parable   10
Passover   16, 17
path   13
Peter   7, 8, 13, 14, 19, 20
Pharisees   1, 14
Philip   6
Pompey   1
Pontius Pilate   18
poor   7, 8, 11, 18
power   1, 9, 11
prayer   11, 17
prefect   6
priest   1, 3, 5, 10, 18, 20
prophet   13, 16

R

rabbi   1, 7, 8, 15
religion, Greek   1
religion, Roman   2
resurrection   19
roads   2
Roman Empire   1, 2, 4, 6, 16, 20
Romans   1, 2, 3, 4, 5, 6, 7, 8, 13, 19
Rome   2

S

sabbath   3, 6, 19
Sadducees   1
Samaria   8, 10
Samaritan   10
Sanhedrin   1, 16
Savior   4
school   6
scourge   18
scribes   1
scriptures   1, 3
shepherd   4, 13
showbread   3
soldiers   2, 5, 17, 18
star   5
stone   6
suffering   12, 13, 18, 19
synagogue   6
Syria   1

T

tax collector   1
taxes   4, 16
teacher   1, 5, 7, 8, 10, 14, 15
temple   3, 5, 6, 7, 16
Thomas   19
tomb   18, 19
trade   3
travel   2

V

vine   13
violence   18

W

water   14
weapons   5
wine   17
wise men   5
wood   6
worship   2

Z

Zealots   1
Zacharias   3, 7
Zion   3